Experiments with Light

Light Energy

Rachel Lynette

Heinemann
LIBRARY

www.heinemann.co.uk/library

Visit our website to find out more information about Heinemann Library books.

To order:

☎ Phone 44 (0) 1865 888066

📄 Send a fax to 44 (0) 1865 314091

🖥 Visit the Heinemann bookshop at **www.heinemann.co.uk/library** to browse our catalogue and order online.

First published in Great Britain by Heinemann Library, Halley Court, Jordan Hill, Oxford OX2 8EJ, part of Pearson Education.

Heinemann is a registered trademark of Pearson Education Ltd.

© Pearson Education Ltd 2008
First published in paperback in 2008
The moral right of the proprietor has been asserted.

Editorial: Louise Galpine and Catherine Veitch
Design: Richard Parker and Tinstar Design Ltd
Illustrations: Oxford designers & illustrators
Picture Research: Hannah Taylor
Production: Victoria Fitzgerald

Originated by Chroma Graphics (Overseas) Pte. Ltd
Printed and bound in China by Leo Paper Group.

ISBN 978 0 431 11128 5 (hardback)
12 11 10 09 08
10 9 8 7 6 5 4 3 2 1

ISBN 978 0 431 11144 5 (paperback)
12 11 10 09 08
10 9 8 7 6 5 4 3 2 1

British Library Cataloguing in Publication Data

Lynette, Rachel
Experiments with light : light energy. – (Do it yourself)
535

A full catalogue record for this book is available from the British Library.

Acknowledgements

We would like to thank the following for permission to reproduce photographs: ©Corbis pp. **7** (Roger Ressmeyer), **9** (Duomo), **10** (Eye Ubiquitous/Adrian Carroll), **15** (zefa/JLP/Jose Luis Pelaez), **19** (zefa/Brigitte Sporrer), **21** (Steve Kaufman), **32** (Robert Glusic), **42** (The Cover Story/Floris Leeuwenberg); ©Ecoscene p. **39** (Chinch Gryniewicz); ©Exploratorium p. **27**; ©Getty Images pp. **17** (Digital Vision), **24** (Chip Simons), **29** (Photographer's Choice), **31** (William Thomas Cain), **33** (VEER John Churchman), **43** (Altrendo Travel); ©istockphoto.com p. **11**; ©Pearson Education Ltd p. **28** (MM Studios); ©Science Faction Images p. **22**; ©Science Photo Library pp. **4** (Ian Vernon), **13** (Jerome Wexler), **14** (David Parker), **25** (HUBBLE HERITAGE TEAM/NASA/ESA/STScI/AURA), **37** (Martin Bond), **41** (Tek Image), **35**; ©TopFoto pp. **23** (UPP, 2004), **34** (Cornell University).

Cover photograph of a torch beam reproduced with permission of ©Corbis/Thom Lang.

We would like to thank Ann Fullick for her invaluable help in the preparation of this book.

Every effort has been made to contact copyright holders of any material reproduced in this book. Any omissions will be rectified in subsequent printings if notice is given to the publishers.

Disclaimer

Contents

Any words appearing in the text in bold, **like this**, are explained in the glossary.

Light energy

Imagine a world with no light. If there were no light, you would not be able to see colours, objects, or anything at all. We need light to see, but, more importantly, we also need light to live! Plants cannot grow without light. All animals, including humans, eat plants, or they eat animals that eat plants. Without light there can be no life on planet Earth.

Our biggest and most important source of light is the Sun. The Sun makes life possible on our planet. The Sun is a natural source of light. Other natural sources of light include lightning and fire. Some animals, such as glowworms and fireflies, can also produce light. In addition to natural light sources, there are also artificial lights made by people. Propane gas lanterns and electric lights are examples of artificial lights.

The Sun is our biggest source of light.

What is light?

Light is a form of energy that travels in waves. It is a form of **electromagnetic radiation**. Light is a part of a huge family of different types of waves known as the **electromagnetic spectrum**. Electromagnetic waves are all around us all the time. Some waves, such as radio waves, are very long, while others, such as X-rays, are very short. Light waves are the only waves that you can see. You see light waves as the colours of the rainbow. Whenever you see colour, you are actually seeing light waves.

Little light waves

Light waves are very short. Over 30,000 of them can fit into 2.54 cm (one inch)!

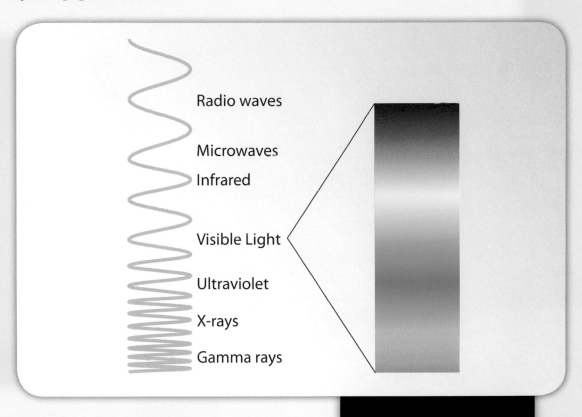

Radio waves

Microwaves

Infrared

Visible Light

Ultraviolet

X-rays

Gamma rays

Light waves are part of the electromagnetic spectrum.

Light speed

Light is the fastest thing in the universe. In space, light travels 299,790 kilometres (186,281 miles) per second. That means that light can travel all the way around the world seven times in less than a second! Even though the Sun is 150 million kilometres (93 million miles) away, it takes just eight minutes for the Sun's light to reach Earth.

Light and dark

Steps to follow

Warning: Be careful with using flour if you are an asthma or coeliac sufferer.

Beam of light

For this activity you will need:
* A torch
* Aluminium foil
* A pin or drawing pin
* A few teaspoons of flour
* A teaspoon
* A dark room
* A table.

1 Cover the top of the torch with aluminium foil so that no light can escape.

2 Use a pin to make a small hole in the centre of the foil.

3 In a dark room, position the torch on a table or counter so that it is facing a blank wall. You should see a tiny circle of light on the wall, but you will not be able to see the beam of light coming from your torch.

4 Take a spoonful of flour and gently blow the flour over the light beam. Can you see the light beam now?

What we see

Most things do not produce their own light. We can only see them because they **reflect** light from a light source. When you made a small circle of light on the wall with your torch, you could see the part of the wall in the circle because it was reflecting the light back to you. If the torch was the only light source in the room, you could not see the rest of the wall. This is because there was no light for it to reflect.

These searchlights show that light always travels in a straight line.

Light travels in a straight line

You cannot see a beam of light. But sometimes you can see light reflecting off **matter** within a light beam. When you blew the flour into the beam, the flour reflected the light, so you could see the beam. Could you see how light travels in a straight line?

Moonlight

The Moon is not actually a light source. The light we see from the Moon is sunlight that is being reflected off the Moon. The Moon looks bright because it is so close to Earth. Without the Sun, we would not be able to see the Moon at all.

Steps to follow

Make a sundial

For this activity you will need:
* A pencil
* Chalk
* Modelling clay or play dough
* A watch
* Sunshine.

1 It is a good idea to start this project early in the morning. Begin by locating a sunny spot on your driveway or a path.

2 Place a ball of clay on the ground, with the pencil sticking straight up in the clay like a flagpole.

3 Use your watch to keep track of the time. Every hour, use the chalk to trace the **shadow** of the pencil. Label each chalk line with the time. By the end of the day, you should have a semi-circle of lines around your pencil.

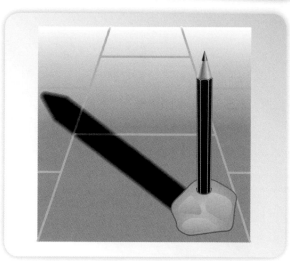

4 Leave the pencil overnight and come back the next morning. The shadow of the pencil is like the hour hand of a clock. Over the course of the day, it will move around the semicircle of chalk lines, telling you what time it is!

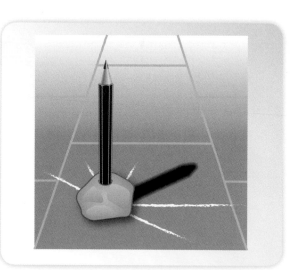

How does it work?

Every day the Sun rises in the east and sets in the west. From Earth, it appears the Sun is travelling in an arc across the sky, but actually, the Sun does not move at all. We are the ones moving. Earth rotates once every 24 hours, making it seem as if the Sun is moving.

Warning: Never look directly at the Sun.

The angle of the Sun makes this boy's shadow long.

The pencil on your sundial blocks the light of the Sun, making a shadow. The part of a sundial that makes a shadow is called the **gnomon**. The shadow moves in a slow semi-circle because the angle of the Sun changes as Earth rotates. You can demonstrate this by shining a torch over a pencil in a dark room and observing the shadow's movement.

Earth rotates on an imaginary **axis**. Imagine a pencil pushed through the centre of an orange. The pencil is the axis. Earth rotates on a tilted axis, so imagine the pencil tilted a little to one side. In addition, when Earth orbits the Sun, it does not move in a circle. Instead, it follows an **elliptical** orbit, so at some times of the year Earth is closer to the Sun than at others. As a result the Sun does not follow the same path across the sky each day. Because the position of the Sun changes, the shadows from the gnomon also change. Many sundials use angled gnomons to help fix this problem.

Something more

Try making a sundial on cardboard. Save your sundial for a few weeks, then try it again in the same spot and mark the hours with a different colour of chalk. Are the lines different? Why are they different?

Before clocks were invented people used sundials to tell the time.

Ancient clocks

Sundials have been used to tell the time for thousands of years. They were used in ancient Egypt, Rome, and China. Early sundials did not divide the day into hours. The earliest sundials simply marked noon when the Sun was directly overhead. Over the centuries, sundials became more precise.

Clockwise

The hands of the first clocks were made to imitate the shadow on a sundial. Since the shadow of a gnomon travels from left to right in the Northern **Hemisphere,** clock hands were made to move in the same direction. This direction became known as clockwise. If clocks had been developed in the Southern Hemisphere, the hands would probably move in the opposite direction or what is currently known as counterclockwise!

This sundial has a slanted gnomon to make it more accurate.

Early clocks were not very accurate. People had to use sundials to set them. Also many people still used sundials because clocks were expensive. It was not until the early 1800s that mechanical clocks could be made cheap enough for most people to use.

Refracting light

Steps to follow

Bending light

For this activity you will need:

* A clear glass, half full of water
* A cardboard shoe box
* White paper
* A torch
* Scissors
* A dark room.

1 Cut two 5-cm (2-in) slits about 2.5 cm (1 in) apart on one end of the box.

2 Put the white paper in the bottom of the box. Place the glass of water in the centre of the box, on top of the white paper.

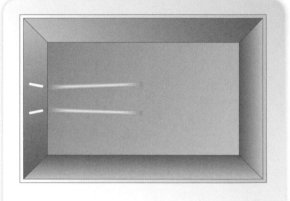

3 In a dark room, shine the torch through the two slits. Look into the box from above. You should see two straight lines of light going into the glass. The lines should bend as they enter the glass and again as they leave the glass. Can you move the glass to make the lines cross?

What happened?

Light can travel through **transparent** substances such as glass and water. However, these substances slow light down. When the light changes speed, it bends. This bending of light is called **refraction**. In your experiment, the light was refracted twice – once when it entered the glass and a second time when it left through the other side.

Broken straw

When you look at a straw in a glass of water from the side, the straw looks like it is broken. This is because the light is refracting. The light that hits the top of the straw is travelling quickly through the air. The light that hits the bottom of the straw is moving more slowly through the water. The water refracts the light. When the straw **reflects** the refracted light, it makes the straw look broken.

This straw is not broken, but the refracting light makes it look like it is.

Refraction in the desert

In very hot weather, people sometimes report seeing **mirages** or pools of water that are not really there. The mirage occurs because the hot sand heats the air just above it. Light from the blue sky above travels at a different speed through this hot air than it does through the colder air above. The different air temperatures refract the light, creating the illusion of water on the ground.

Lenses

People use **lenses** to refract light. A lens is a curved piece of transparent material such as glass or plastic. The curve of the lens refracts light to make things appear larger or smaller.

These two lenses bend the light in different ways.

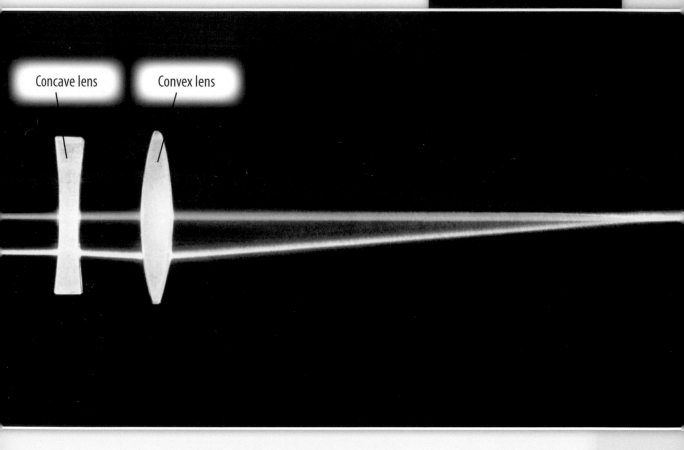

Concave lens

Convex lens

There are two types of lens. **Convex lenses** are thicker in the middle than they are on the edges. Convex lenses bend the light beams towards each other. This makes objects appear bigger. A magnifying glass is an example of a convex lens. **Concave lenses** are thicker on the edges than they are in the middle. They spread the light beams out. Concave lenses make things look smaller. They are usually used in glasses for correcting vision problems.

You can use your box with the two slits to see how different lenses refract light. Ask an adult to help you find some lenses around the house. Magnifying glasses have lenses. What does the light do when you shine it through the lenses you found? What if you use two lenses together?

Lenses for life

Convex lenses are more common than concave ones. Convex lenses are used in cameras, binoculars, and microscopes to magnify objects. The lenses in microscopes are very powerful. They can magnify things up to 1,500 times! Large convex lenses are also used in lighthouses to magnify the light, so that faraway ships can see it.

This microscope uses convex lenses to magnify.

Make a water lens

If you do not have a magnifying glass, you can use a drop of water! Just put a drop of water on a piece of stiff, transparent plastic such as the lid from a clear plastic container. Now position the drop over a newspaper or magazine. The drop of water is curved, so it acts like a convex lens and magnifies the words. Try different sizes of drops. What if you used a drop of baby oil?

Your eyes have lenses, too!

In your eye the lens is located just behind the **pupil**. Your pupils get bigger and smaller to control the amount of light that gets into your eyes. You can test this by going into a dark room for a few minutes and then turning on a light. Look in a mirror. Your pupils will be big because they were trying to help you see in the dark by allowing as much light in as possible. Within a few seconds, your pupils will get smaller. When the light is bright, your pupils do not need to let as much in.

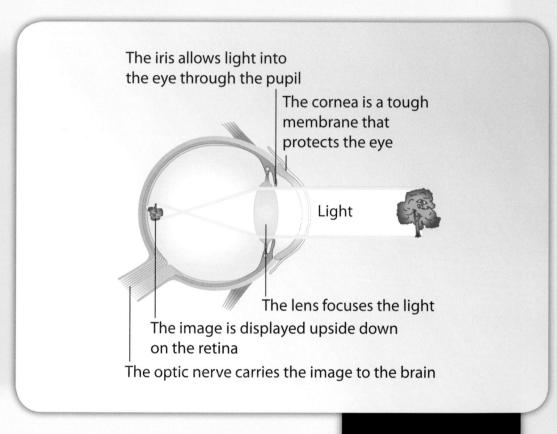

The iris allows light into the eye through the pupil

The cornea is a tough membrane that protects the eye

Light

The lens focuses the light

The image is displayed upside down on the retina

The optic nerve carries the image to the brain

The light that is reflected from objects goes through your pupil and then through the lens in your eye. An image of the object falls on the **retina** at the back of your eye. The retina is like a cinema screen, except that the image is displayed upside down. The reason the image is upside down is because your eye is curved. Your eye sends the picture to the brain, where it is interpreted as being the right way up. You can see how a curved surface can turn an image upside down by looking at your reflection in a spoon.

Light travels through your eye's lens to the retina.

Correcting vision

The lenses in your eyes change shape all the time, getting thicker or thinner so you can see things clearly. When you get older, the lens can become more rigid, so it does not change shape as easily. Sometimes, the shape changes permanently, causing vision problems. Eyeglasses can help fix these problems. **Nearsighted** people have trouble seeing things that are far away. They need concave lenses. **Farsighted** people have the opposite problem. They have trouble seeing things that are close up. They need convex lenses.

Many people wear glasses or contact lenses to correct vision problems.

Digital cameras

A digital camera works in a similar way to your eyes. The image is focused through the lens and recorded digitally in the camera.

Reflecting light

Steps to follow

1 Cut the index card so that you have a right-angle triangle with two sides that are each 7.6 cm (3 in) long.

2 Line up the right angle of the triangle card with one corner of the box and trace the diagonal side to make a line.

3 Line up the card in the opposite corner of the same side to make another diagonal line. The two lines should be parallel.

4 Ask an adult to use the knife to cut slits where your lines are.

Warning: Adult help is needed for this experiment.

More of this activity to come on page 20.

Make a periscope

For this activity you will need:
* A long, skinny box, like the type of box kitchen foil comes in, taped closed
* Two small mirrors (you can often find these where make-up is sold)
* A 7.6 x 12.7 cm (3 x 5 in) index card
* A pen
* Scissors
* A knife.

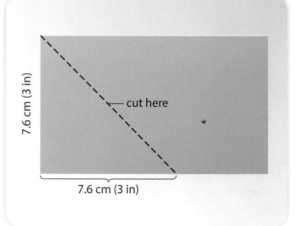

7.6 cm (3 in)

cut here

7.6 cm (3 in)

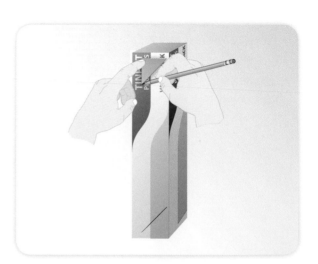

How mirrors work

Most objects **absorb** some light and **reflect** some light. The light that they reflect goes in many different directions. But smooth, shiny surfaces, such as mirrors, reflect all of the light waves at the same angle that they hit. That is why you see your own reflection and other images in a mirror.

This mirrored disco ball is reflecting tiny squares of light on the wall.

Marvellous mirrors

You probably look in a mirror every morning when you brush your hair. But mirrors are not just for helping you make sure you do not go to school with messy hair. Cars are equipped with rearview mirrors as well as side mirrors so that drivers can see what is behind them. Dentists use small mirrors to get a good look at their patients' teeth. Interior decorators often use mirrors to make a space look bigger. Have you ever looked closely at a disco ball? It is covered with hundreds of tiny mirrors!

5 Use your triangle to draw two more lines on the other side of the box. These lines should line up evenly with the lines on the other side. Ask an adult to make the lines into slits with a knife.

8 You can use your **periscope** to see around corners or over people's heads in a crowd. Just aim the square hole at the top at what you want to see and look through the hole near the bottom.

6 Push one of the mirrors through the slits on the bottom of your box. Most of the mirror should be inside the box, with the edges sticking out of the slits. The mirror should be facing up into the box. Push the second mirror through the slits at the top of the box. This mirror should be facing the bottom mirror.

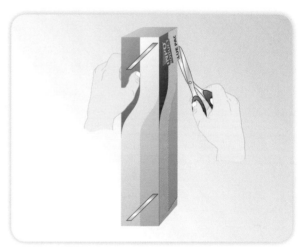

7 Cut a large square near the top of the box. You should be able to see the shiny side of the top mirror through the square. Use a pen to make a small hole on the opposite side of the box near the bottom. You should be able to see the shiny side of the bottom mirror through this hole.

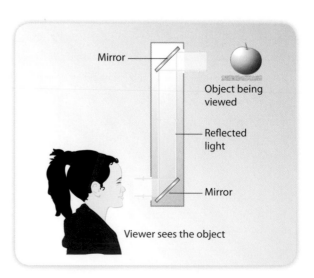

Mirror

Object being viewed

Reflected light

Mirror

Viewer sees the object

How does your periscope work?

A periscope works by reflecting light. Light is reflected from objects through the square hole and onto the top mirror. The top mirror is angled to reflect the light through the periscope and onto the bottom mirror. The bottom mirror is angled to reflect the light through the hole and into your eyes, so that you can see the objects.

This man is using a periscope in a submarine to see above the surface of the water.

Periscopes in wartime

Periscopes were used in World War I (1914–1918) and World War II (1939–1945). Submarines could stay hidden under the water while a periscope was raised to find and target enemy ships. These periscopes often had magnifying **lenses** to increase their range.

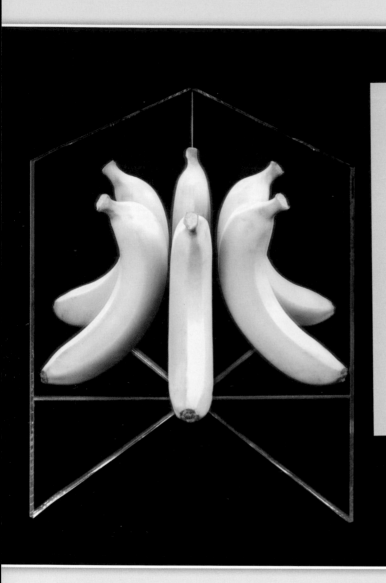

Fun with mirrors

Get two mirrors that are the same size. Ask an adult to help you tape them together along one edge, like an open book. The shiny sides should face inwards. Stand your mirrors on a table and position them into a "V" shape. Place an object, such as a banana, between the mirrors. How many reflections of the banana do you see? Can you change the angle of the mirrors so that you can see even more reflections of the banana?

In angled mirrors you can see your reflection many times because the light bounces back and forth between them. Every time the light hits one of the mirrors, it reflects your image. When you make the angle between the mirrors smaller, the light bounces more times, and you see more images of yourself.

Now separate your mirrors. Hold them upright, about 30 centimetres (12 inches) apart and facing each other. Look into one of the mirrors from the side. If you can position yourself in just the right way, you can see that your image is repeated endlessly. This happens because the light bounces back and forth between the mirrors, making reflections of reflections.

Mirror mazes

Have you ever been in a maze of mirrors? Small ones can sometimes be found at funfairs. Mirror mazes use many mirrors to confuse visitors. There are beautiful and elaborate mirror mazes in many places throughout the world. One of the first mirror mazes was built in 1896. It is located in Lucerne, Switzerland, and contains 90 mirrors.

This woman is trying to find her way through a mirror maze.

Animals and mirrors

Most animals do not recognize themselves in mirrors. Instead, they think that their reflection is another animal. Animals that do recognize themselves include dolphins, elephants, and some kinds of primates, such as great apes and chimpanzees.

Mirrors and telescopes

Powerful telescopes use giant mirrors to collect light from distant objects such as planets and stars. These mirrors are curved like a shallow bowl and are called **parabolic reflectors**. The curved surface makes it possible to collect a lot of light and **focus** it onto a smaller surface. This focused light is reflected onto a much smaller mirror. The smaller mirror is angled to reflect the light into the eyepiece of the telescope.

The telescopes in **observatories** must have very large mirrors in order to collect enough light to see things that are very far away. The mirrors must be shaped exactly right or the image will be blurred. These mirrors can take months to grind and polish. They are the most expensive part of the telescope, costing millions of pounds.

This astronomer is looking into a liquid mirror telescope.

Liquid mirrors

A new technology involves making telescope mirrors by spinning liquid **mercury** in a parabola-shaped dish. These **liquid mirrors** cost only a fraction of the price of traditional parabolic reflectors and work just as well. However, these mirrors cannot be tilted, or the mercury will spill out of the dish. This means that telescopes with liquid mirrors cannot move to track objects as Earth rotates.

This picture of newly formed stars was taken by the Hubble Space Telescope.

The Hubble Space Telescope

The National Aeronautics and Space Administration (NASA) designed the Hubble Space Telescope to look at the universe from space. It was launched on 24 April 1990. It travels at a speed of 8 kilometres (5 miles) per second. It orbits Earth once every 97 minutes.

The mirror in the Hubble Space Telescope measures 2.4 metres (7.9 feet) across and took over a year to grind and polish. However, it became clear that there was a problem with the mirror soon after the telescope was launched. The pictures it took were blurred. The problem was a tiny flaw with the shape of the mirror. The mistake was only about one-fiftieth of the thickness of a sheet of paper. Engineers worked out how to fix the problem with a series of small mirrors. Astronauts made the repairs as the telescope orbited Earth.

Light and colour

Steps to follow

1 Trace the heads of the torches on the report covers and cut out one circle of each colour. These will be your colour **filters**. Tape a filter to each torch so that each torch shines a different colour of light.

2 Take your friends and your torches into a dark room. Shine the beams against a white wall. Cross two of the beams so that the colours mix. What colour did you get? Try more combinations. Can you get **white light** by combining all three of the colours?

Mixing light

For this activity you will need:
* Three torches
* Transparent plastic report covers or file folders in blue, green, and red
* A pen or pencil
* Scissors
* Clear tape
* A dark room
* Two friends.

Focusing the light

If the colours are not mixing well, you can focus the lights by making tubes for the torches. Tubes from empty kitchen paper rolls might fit over the heads of your torches. If not, make tubes from stiff paper and tape.

Make colourful shadows

Ask one of your friends to hold the torches. Put your hand in the beams close to the wall. Try to put your hand in front of just one beam. Get your friends to experiment with moving the torches. What colour **shadows** can you make?

When you put your hand in front of one of the coloured beams of light, it makes a shadow. But because you are not blocking the other two colours, they mix together and make a coloured shadow. Can you position your hand to make three different shadows? How many colours can you make?

You can make bigger shadows by asking an adult to buy and assemble three floodlights with red, blue, and green light bulbs. Position the lights so all three combine against the wall. Have fun making big, beautiful, coloured shadows with your whole body!

You can use the three primary colours of light to make colourful shadows.

The three primary colours of light

Red, blue, and green are the three **primary colours** of light. All other colours can be made from these three colours. Mixing two of them together may give you some surprising results. Mixing light is not like mixing paint. When you mix light waves together, you are adding the colours. The more colours you combine, the more light waves you have. As you saw with your filtered torches, when you add all three of them together, you get white light.

This car looks yellow because it is reflecting yellow light waves.

Colour confusion

You may be feeling confused because your art teacher told you that the three primary colours are red (sometimes called magenta), blue (sometimes called cyan), and yellow. You have probably also learned that when you mix all these colours together you get black, not white. What is going on? The primary colours for light sources are different from the primary colours for paint, ink, crayons, and other **pigments** that do not create their own light.

Computer colour

All the colours on your computer screen are made from only the three primary colours of light. The pictures you see are made up of millions of tiny **pixels**. Each pixel contains the three primary colours. The pixels are put together in different ways to make the colours you see.

You already know that you can see objects because they **reflect** light. Objects also **absorb** light. If you paint a toy car blue, the pigments in the blue paint absorb all of the light waves except the blue ones. The blue ones are reflected off the car, and so the car looks blue. When you mix paint colours, more light waves are being absorbed and fewer are being reflected, so you are actually taking colour away. That is why you get black when you mix all the colours. When something is black, it is not reflecting any light.

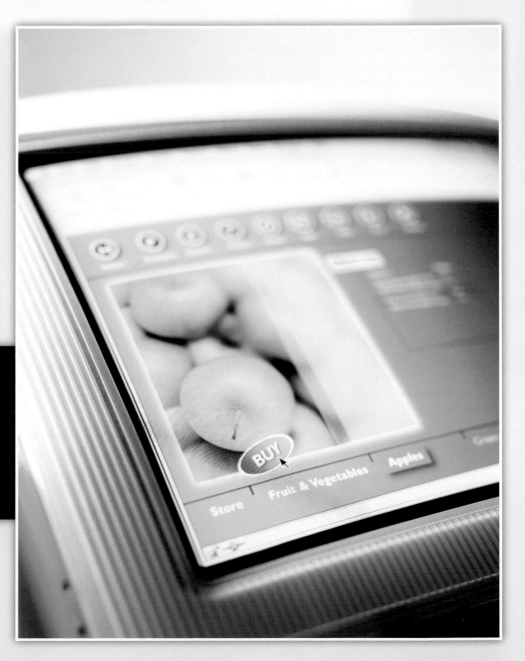

Pixels have been used to make the colours you see on this computer screen.

The colours we see

Steps to follow

Is a red apple always red?

For this activity you will need:

* A cardboard shoe box
* Two **transparent** plastic report covers in green and red (coloured cellophane will also work)
* Tape
* Scissors
* A torch
* A lemon, a green pepper, and a red apple.

1 Cut a large rectangle in the top of the shoe box lid and a smaller rectangle on one end.

2 Cut out a rectangular piece of red plastic that is slightly bigger than the rectangular hole that you cut in the top of the box. Tape the red plastic rectangle over the rectangular hole.

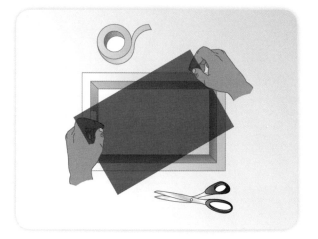

3 Put the coloured objects in the box. Put the lid back on and shine the torch through the hole on the end. Look through the red rectangle on the lid. What do you see? Take the red plastic off the lid and try the same experiment with the green plastic. What if you use both colours on top of each other?

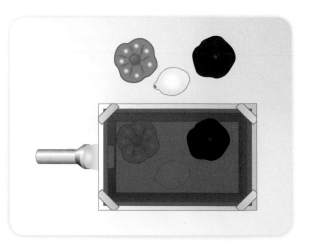

What is happening?

When you used the red **filter**, only red light got to the objects in your box. That meant that the colour of the apple did not change much because the **pigment** in the skin of the apple **reflects** red light. There was plenty of red light coming through the filter. But it did not work that way for the other two things in your box. The green pepper normally reflects green light waves, but with the red filter, there were very few green light waves for the pepper to reflect. This caused the pepper to turn brown. The red filter also changed the colour of the lemon, making it look more like an orange!

One-colour world

Use your plastic report covers to make yourself some coloured glasses. Cut frames from cardboard or twist them out of pipe cleaners. Cut the plastic report covers into the right shapes and tape or glue them onto the frames of your glasses. What is it like to live in a blue world? How about a green one?

This man's glasses filter the light so he sees everything with a red tint.

What is a rainbow?

When you see a rainbow, you are seeing **white light** from the Sun separated into seven colours. The white light from the Sun is **refracted** and reflected by raindrops. The curved surface of the drops refracts each colour light wave at a slightly different angle and reflects the colour outwards. The waves are refracted at different angles because each colour has its own **wavelength**. Violet waves are the shortest, while on the other end of the spectrum, red waves are the longest.

Make a rainbow

Take a CD and a strong torch into a dark room. Shine the torch on the shiny side of the CD. If you get the angle right, you should see the colours of the rainbow on the CD. Now move the torch to try to get the light to reflect a rainbow from the CD to the wall or the ceiling.

Just like a raindrop, the grooves in the CD refract the light and separate the different colour waves so that you see the individual colours. The CD is shiny, so it reflects the light onto the ceiling or wall.

A rainbow is actually white light refracted into seven colours.

Blue skies and sunsets

The sky looks blue because the Sun produces a lot of blue light waves. Since blue waves are very short, they scatter easily in Earth's atmosphere, making the sky appear blue. The Sun does not make many violet light waves, so even though violet light waves are shorter than blue light waves, the sky does not look violet.

We see a beautiful sunset when orange and red light waves reflect off matter in the air.

We see orange sunsets because orange and red light waves are very long, and so they do not scatter. Instead, they reflect off the **matter** that is in the atmosphere. We see the colours at sunset because at that time of day the Sun is far away on the **horizon** and the light waves travel a longer distance to our eyes. On their way to us, the orange and red light waves encounter a lot of matter that it can reflect off. That is what we see when we see a beautiful orange sunset.

Ultraviolet light

You have probably heard about **ultraviolet light**, sometimes called UV light. Ultraviolet light waves are even shorter than violet light waves. They are just beyond violet waves on the **electromagnetic spectrum**, so we cannot see them.

Ultraviolet waves are dangerous to people. They can cause sunburn as well as skin cancer and damage to the eyes. Earth's atmosphere protects us from most of the ultraviolet light that the Sun gives off, but some does get through. It is important to protect yourself from ultraviolet light waves by wearing sun lotion and sunglasses.

This ultraviolet picture of a flower is how scientists believe some insects see.

There are many technologies that use ultraviolet light. Important documents such as passports, credit cards, and even banknotes often have invisible images printed on them. These images can only be seen under an ultraviolet light (sometimes called a black light) so that fake documents can be detected. Ultraviolet light can also be used for **sterilizing** water and medical equipment.

Infrared light

Like ultraviolet light waves, **infrared light** waves are also invisible to humans. These waves lie just beyond red light waves on the electromagnetic spectrum. They are slightly longer than red light waves.

Scientists have also discovered many ways to use infrared light waves. Infrared light waves can be used to make and detect heat. One common use is in night vision equipment. Night vision goggles and other viewers work by detecting heat. Infrared light can also be used as a heat source. Infrared light is used to de-ice aeroplane wings and to heat tarmac during road construction. In addition, most remote controls use infrared lights to send a code to a device such as a television. The television has a receiver that decodes the message.

Animal eyesight

People cannot see infrared or ultraviolet light, but scientists have evidence that many animals can. Reptiles can see infrared light, and some insects can see ultraviolet light.

This picture was taken using infrared technology.

Light power

Steps to follow

1 Draw a large square on the lid of the pizza box. Cut along three sides to make a flap. The back of the flap should be at the back of the box.

2 Put foil on the underside of the flap with the shiny side out. Try not to wrinkle it. Then cover the inside of the box with foil. Use tape or glue to secure the foil.

3 Put a piece of black construction paper on top of the foil on the bottom of your box.

Warning: Adult help is needed for this experiment.

More of this activity to come on page 38.

Make a solar oven

For this activity you will need:

* A flat box, such as an unused pizza box
* A pen or pencil
* Scissors
* Kitchen foil
* Clingfilm
* Black construction paper
* Non-toxic tape and glue
* A stick
* A biscuit, a marshmallow, and a piece of chocolate
* Sunshine and warm weather (it does not need to be hot, but you should be able to be outside in short sleeves.)

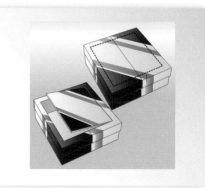

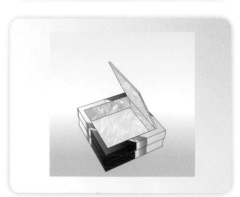

Solar cooking around the world

Solar ovens are great for people living in underdeveloped countries. Countries in Africa, Asia, and South America get a great deal of Sun, so there is plenty of power for their ovens. Many people in these countries are very poor. Solar ovens are not expensive. Using the Sun to cook means that people do not have to spend time gathering wood or use what little money they have to buy fuel. In addition, solar ovens do not need a fire to work, so they do not make smoke and cause pollution.

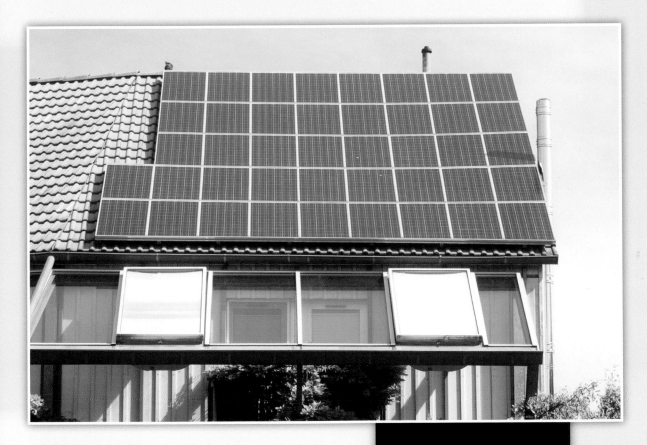

Solar energy

Energy from the Sun can be used for much more than cooking. By using **solar panels**, light energy can be converted to electrical energy, which can then be used in many different ways. Some people use large solar collectors to power their whole house! Solar power is **renewable**, which means it will never run out. In addition, it does not cause pollution.

The solar panels on this house convert energy from the Sun into electricity.

4 Cut a piece of clingfilm a little bigger than the flap on the lid. Tape it to the underside of the lid so that it covers the square hole. Tape it tightly closed so that no air can get inside. Your solar oven is finished!

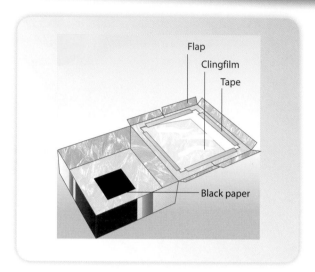

Flap
Clingfilm
Tape
Black paper

5 Only use your solar oven with adult supervision! Put half of a biscuit on the black paper with a square of chocolate and a marshmallow on top. Close the lid and prop the flap up with the stick so that the angle **reflects** sunlight into your oven.

6 It may take a while for your marshmallow to cook. Watch it carefully and reposition the oven if necessary. Be careful – the marshmallow will get hot! When it is done, ask an adult to carefully take the biscuit and marshmallow out of the solar oven. Add another biscuit and enjoy your snack!

How does a solar oven work?

Solar ovens convert light from the Sun into heat. The shiny parts of the oven reflect light waves from the Sun into the box where your food is. The black paper **absorbs** the light and converts it to heat. The heat stays trapped in the box and cooks the food. This means that it does not need to be hot outside to use a solar oven, but it does need to be sunny.

These people in Tibet are using a solar cooker.

More solar cooking

You may want to put an oven thermometer inside your oven to see how hot it gets. Be sure to position the thermometer so that you can read it through the plastic window. Experiment with improving your solar oven. Can you add more reflectors to direct more sunlight inside? Is there a way to add **insulation** to keep the heat inside? Insulation is especially important if it is not a hot day.

What else can you cook? Try melting cheese to make a sandwich or nachos. Can you heat water to make hot chocolate? Will your oven get hot enough to bake biscuits?

Lasers

You have probably seen low-power **laser** pointers. Lasers are made by intensifying the waves from just one colour of light. This makes the light very powerful and very precise. Lasers can be strong enough to **vaporize** metal. They are often used in factories to **weld** or separate plastic or metal. Lasers are also accurate enough to be used by doctors in delicate surgeries.

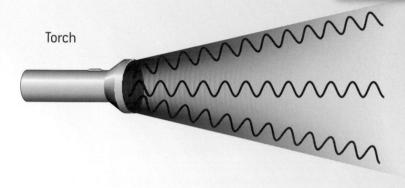

Torch

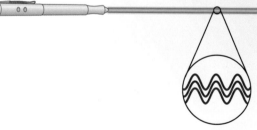

Laser pointer

Light waves from a torch scatter from the source. However, light waves from a laser are more concentrated.

There are probably lasers in your home. Lasers are used in DVD players. DVDs are imprinted with digital information in the form of microscopic ridges. In a DVD player, a laser reflects off these ridges onto a special receiver. A DVD player can read these reflections and turn them into pictures and sounds, so you can watch films. A similar technology is used to play CDs.

Fibre optics

Lasers are also used in **fibre optics**. Fibre optics are long, thin strands of glass that carry coded information in the form of laser light. A fibre optic strand is thinner than a human hair. These strands are usually made of glass that is surrounded by a reflective coating. The light does not escape from the glass strand because it continually bounces off the reflective coating. Thousands of fibre optic strands are grouped together in bundles to make a fibre optic cable. Fibre optic strands can carry much more information than electrical wires. They can be used to carry telephone communications, TV broadcasts, and computer data.

The first laser

In 1960 the first working laser was demonstrated by US physicist Theodore Maiman in Malibu, California, USA. The word "laser" is actually an **acronym** for "Light Amplification by Stimulated Emission of Radiation".

Fibre optic strands like these can carry a great deal of information.

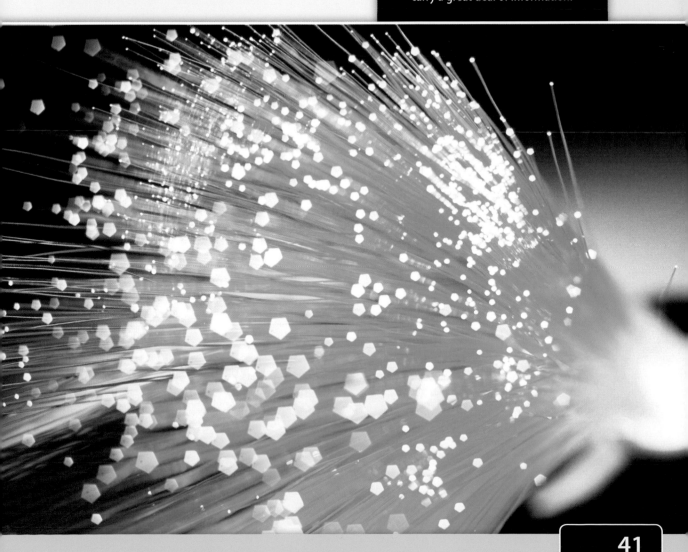

Light in our lives

Light lets us see the world around us, but it also does much more. Light is essential for using all kinds of tools and toys, from microscopes to kaleidoscopes. By understanding light waves, scientists have been able to create many technologies to help people and to help us learn about our world.

By **refracting** and **reflecting** light, it is possible for us to observe the tiniest micro-organisms. That same technology helps us to study giant stars located far from our own solar system. Even something as simple as a pair of spectacles could not be made if people did not understand how light can be refracted.

This giant mirror traps the Sun's rays to make steam for cooking.

Scientists have even found ways to use the light waves that we cannot see. **Ultraviolet light** has become a valuable tool for **sterilizing** food and medical equipment. **Infrared light** makes it possible for you to turn your television off without also turning your neighbour's television off.

Light up your life

Some people feel depressed when they are not exposed to much natural light, especially in the winter. Sunshine makes them feel better.

A bright future

Scientists continue to find new and exciting ways to use light. Today, more than ever, it is important to find ways to make electricity without harming the planet. With concerns about dwindling oil reserves and global warming, solar power from the Sun is a promising technology for the future. Because it is **renewable** and it does not cause pollution, more people are using solar power than ever before!

Another exciting technology is **LEDs** (light emitting diodes). These little lights use much less electricity than other bulbs. They are used in the displays for electronic devices as well as in traffic lights and in giant television screens. Many people also have LED party lights. Because they use so little electricity, LEDs will probably someday replace traditional light bulbs in houses, schools, and businesses.

Glossary

absorb soak up or take in. Most objects absorb some light waves.

acronym word formed from the initial letters of other words

axis centre around which something rotates

concave lens lens that is thicker on the edges than it is in the middle and is used to make things appear smaller

convex lens lens that is thicker in the middle than it is on the edges and is used to make things appear larger. The convex lens in a magnifying glass is good for examining fingerprints.

electromagnetic radiation form of energy that travels in waves. The light we see is a form of electromagnetic radiation.

electromagnetic spectrum range of energy waves from the shortest to the longest. Radio waves and microwaves are part of the electromagnetic spectrum.

elliptical oval or egg-shaped path. Earth travels in an elliptical orbit round the Sun.

farsighted able to see distant objects more clearly than close ones

fibre optics long, thin strands of glass that carry coded information in the form of light

filter device that removes something from whatever passes through it. A light filter absorbs some light waves, while letting others pass through it.

focus make something appear clear and sharp. The lens in your eye automatically focuses so that you can see clearly.

gnomon upright part of a sundial that casts a shadow. You can use a flagpole as a gnomon if you trace the shadow it makes each hour.

horizon where the land and sky appear to meet

hemisphere one half of the Earth

infrared light energy waves that are longer than visible light waves and shorter than radio waves. The remote control for your TV probably uses infrared light waves.

insulation material that prevents the passage of heat, sound, or electricity. The insulation in the walls of your house helps to keep the heat inside.

laser tightly focused beam of light that has only one wavelength

LED (light emitting diode) small light that uses less electricity than traditional bulbs

lens curved piece of glass or plastic used to bend light. You can use a clear marble as a lens.

liquid mirror mirror that is made by spinning liquid metal in a shallow, dish-shaped container at high speeds. Liquid mirrors can measure several metres across!

matter anything that has weight and takes up space. Everything you see, including yourself, is made from matter.

mercury heavy, silvery, and poisonous metallic element that is liquid at room temperature. You should never touch, inhale, or eat mercury.

mirage optical illusion caused by light bending when it passes through hot and cold air

nearsighted able to see close objects more clearly than distant ones

observatory place with a telescope and other equipment to view objects in space. Science museums often have observatories for learning about the universe.

parabolic reflector round, dish-shaped mirror that is large enough to collect light and shaped in such a way that it can focus the light. A telescope in Hawaii has a giant parabolic reflector that is nearly 10 metres (33 feet) across.

periscope long tube that uses mirrors to let viewers see objects that are not in the direct line of sight. You can use a periscope to watch television from behind the couch!

pigment substance that soaks up some light waves and reflect others to give something its colour

pixel tiny dot of light that joins with other dots to make up an image on a computer or television screen. A digital picture with a lot of pixels will be sharper than one with fewer pixels.

primary colour one of three colours that can be combined to make all other colours. The three primary colours of light are red, blue, and green.

pupil dark circle in the centre of the eye that allows light in. Your eyes take a few minutes to adjust to the dark because the pupils need to get bigger to let more light in.

reflect bounce off something. You can use a mirror to reflect light onto the ceiling.

refract when light bends as it passes from one substance to another. A fish swimming in a fishbowl looks bigger than it really is because the light refracts.

renewable something that does not run out or that can be replaced easily. Solar power from the Sun is renewable because we will never run out of sunlight in our lifetime.

retina layer of cells at the back of the eye that receives images. Your retina is a bit like a cinema screen.

shadow dark shape that falls behind something or someone that is blocking the light. You can use a torch to make large shadows on a blank wall.

solar panel collection of devices that absorb sunlight and turn it into electricity

sterilize make something free of bacteria so diseases cannot be spread. Infrared lights can be used to sterilize water so it is safe to drink.

transparent something that is clear and lets light pass through it

ultraviolet light energy waves that are shorter than visible light waves and longer than X-rays

vaporize turn into a gas. Some lasers are strong enough to vaporize metal!

wavelength Length of a wave when it is measured from one peak to the next. Red light waves have longer wavelengths than blue ones.

weld join together two materials, especially metals, by heating them. Lasers can be used to weld iron.

white light light that contains all the colours of light, which together make the light white

ELIN	
Z771863	
PETERS	23-Mar-2011
535	£8.99

Find out more

Books

Light (*Science View*), Steve Parker
   (New York: Chelsea House, 2005)

A colourful book with information about light and ideas for projects.

Light (*The KidHaven Science Library*), Bonnie Juettner
   (San Diego, Calif.: KidHaven, 2004)

Information about light and how it is used. Includes colour pictures and a glossary.

Light and Colour (*Young Scientists Investigate*), Malcolm Dixon, Karen Smith
   (Evans Publishing, 2005)

Explanations, illustrations and experiments.

Light and Dark (*It's Science*), Sally Hewitt
   (Franklin Watts, 2007)

Looks at science that surrounds us in our everyday world.

Websites

http://www.nasa.gov/worldbook/hubble_telescope_worldbook.html

Learn about NASA's powerful space telescope, the Hubble telescope.

http://www.bbc.co.uk/schools/scienceclips/ages/7_8/light_shadows.shtml

Try activities at the BBC website that test your knowledge of light and shadows.

Organizations

National Aeronautics and Space Administration (NASA)

NASA Headquarters
Suite 5K39
Washington, D.C. 20546-0001
(202) 358-0001
www.nasa.gov/home

NASA's official website contains information about its many programmes, including the Hubble Space Telescope.

Places to visit

The Science Museum

Exhibition Road
South Kensington
London SW7 2DD

http://www.sciencemuseum.org.uk/

Explore the properties of Light at the Science Museum's Light table.

National Media Museum

Bradford,
West Yorkshire,
BD1 1NQ

http://www.nationalmediamuseum.org.uk/

Learn all about the role of light in photography, cinema, and television.

The Royal Observatory, Greenwich

National Maritime Museum
Park Row
Greenwich
London SE10 9NF

www.rog.nmm.ac.uk

Explore the world of telescopes and astronomical observation.

Index